SELFWOLF

PHOENIX **POETS**

A SERIES EDITED BY ALAN SHAPIRO

MARK HALLIDAY

Selfwolf

THE UNIVERSITY OF CHICAGO PRESS
Chicago and London

Mark Halliday is assistant professor English at Ohio University. He is the author of two previous books of poetry, *Little Star*, selected for the National Poetry Series, and *Tasker Street*, winner of the Juniper Prize. He is also author of the critical work *Stevens and the Interpersonal*.

The University of Chicago Press, Chicago 60637
The University of Chicago Press, Ltd., London
© 1999 by The University of Chicago
All rights reserved. Published 1999

08 07 06 05 04 03 02 01 00 99   1 2 3 4 5

ISBN 0-226-31383-2 (cloth)
   0-226-31384-0 (paper)

Halliday, Mark, 1949–
      Selfwolf / Mark Halliday.
            p.   cm. — (Phoenix poets)
      ISBN 0-226-31383-2 (alk. paper). — ISBN 0-226-31384-0 (pbk. :
alk. paper)
      I. Title.   II. Series
PS3558.A386S4 1999
811'.54—dc21   98-19299
                                                                    CIP

Contents

II

III

Acknowledgments

Grateful acknowledgment is made to all of the editors of publications in which these poems, or versions of them, first appeared:

Agni: "Pages," "Pasco, Barbara"
Boston Phoenix: "The Halls" (31 October 1997 issue of the "Phoenix Literary Section")
Chelsea: "Narragansett Boulevard"
Chicago Review: "Horrible"
Cimarron Review: "Alley Sketch" (reprinted with permission of the Board of Regents for Oklahoma State University, holders of the copyright)
Crazyhorse: "Loaded Inflections," "The Miles of Night"
Denver Quarterly: "The Ivory Novel"
Gettysburg Review: "The Case against Mist"
Gulf Coast: "Novelists of 2007"
Indiana Review: "Bad People," "Taipei Tangle"
Paris Review: "Skirt"
Third Coast: "Timberwolf"
Virginia Quarterly Review: "Poetry Friendship on Earth," "Removal Service Request," "Threads"

The Miles of Night

Back from the hospital again, my mother wants us
to share something, so we're all gathered in the downstairs den
for *Long Day's Journey Into Night*, a TV special—
my brother and I understand this is serious art
and our sharing this serious art will be sharing on a high level.
Except for the black-and-white screen, the den is dark.

My father helps my mother get comfortable on the sofa.
"Cancer cannot stop me from appreciating serious art"
is what her fragile comfort (two pillows just so) declares—
"cannot stop me from enjoying serious art
with my family." The acting is so good,
my father keeps saying, and my brother and I keep agreeing

as the ravaged black-and-white screen family keeps reaching
glimpses of their love for each other and then
blasting each other with shame, envy, hate. At least
we're not like *that*; at least we're not like that.
When a commercial comes I climb to the kitchen
and cut four slices of Sara Lee cake though I know

Mom won't eat hers; the kitchen is brazenly bright with color
so I feel like a deserter so I hurry the dessert back down
to the room of serious black and white. Down:
nothing ever goes anywhere but down—but I should keep down
this feeling because we are sharing some serious art
and the acting is so good. The mother is played by Constance Cummings,

an actress apparently admired by my parents in the past—
she holds up her hands like lobster claws
to indicate severe disability
and I'm embarrassed by the obvious metaphor,
obvious in the play and obvious here outside the damn play
so I try to throw my mind out of our dark den

and when the next commercial comes—ABC has an upcoming
special called "Making Good in America"—I go up
for more cake and my brother too shows up—
"Long Day's Booze Into Snooze" he mutters about the serious art
but we think Mom is almost almost happy
and we almost know she'll be dead in eighteen months or less,

less, so soon we're back down saying the acting is so good.
On top of the TV there's this brass fish, it curves
as if yearning upward; and outside there's a dark highway
and on the highway there is a truck
and the driver of the truck for some reason
releases two blasts of his horn

into the miles of night. Image
of courage or futility or both, and my mind prefers
such a clean cold image to our complicated indoor warmth
and so cherishes it for nearly a minute—"the miles of night"—
that I miss something wrenching in Act Four
as well as something soft my mother says or doesn't say.

The Case against Mist

He could not be just particles of mist
dispersing into the sky, he could not be only that
and there are many reasons.
There are some reasons why.

For example, he paddled a canoe down the Housatonic River
for nineteen miles
and learned to keep up with some considerably stronger boys
and then they all laughed together over blueberry pancakes
and that is a reason why.

Also he wrote quite unhappily about the failure of Reconstruction
during the presidency of Ulysses S. Grant,
frowning at the exam booklet in a hot overlit room,
forming complete sentences though he could not remember
anything about Jay Gould, sincerely wishing
he could remember more facts
and sincerely sorry to disappoint Mr. Bennett
and this would not be true if he were simply
particles of mist drifting up into the infinite sky
and so that is why.

Also he never forgot the pathos of sexual fear
which would always link a certain song by Fontella Bass
with a certain large girl in a stiff green dress

in an old Volvo on such a dark highway near Rowayton.
Clearly, thus, he could not be just particles of mist.
The proof is right there.

Besides, his mother sang "Let's go together, says Pooh to me,
let's go together says Pooh" and she sang this
just for him in a voice better than anything else.
So there is a huge proof.

Not to mention that he showed real kindness
to some lonely and troubled individuals
in several houses, lobbies, cafeterias, train stations and
municipal parks, probably to more than 20 percent
of those lonely and anxious individuals that he actually met
in those places during his long busy life, true kindness
with money or food, or talk, or at least thoughtful gestures
and all this constitutes another reason why,
why he could in no way be just mist, vapor, molecules
well on their way to dispersion and nothing else.

We see thus that the proofs are many
and still more could be adduced,
though any one of them should have been enough.

Narragansett Boulevard

On Narragansett Boulevard there is
a black gas tank with iron stairs on it.
One could climb these stairs on a rainy night

and stand cold on the black top
and be there, located in that location
as an option, staring over wet black lots.

Further along Narragansett Boulevard
there is a red oil truck beside a shed
and a weak bulb attached to the tin shed

yellows the dark red of the back of the truck.
One could go there and stand there
in that small light behind the oil truck

for seven hours or eight hours of night
as an option, in that barely lit location.
And there are many other things one could do

on Narragansett Boulevard and anywhere,
rather than be just not there;
climb and stand and stare.

But would there ever be development?
Must there not be development?
You have to develop: you can't choose

not to choose; you have to want,
you have to seek and prefer;
no version of "you" can be nearly nothing

in the chain-link black wet lots on Narragansett;
no option is left for you outside development.

Credentials

He has never lost a child. He has never even
almost lost a child. How can he talk about loss?
He has never been raped. Not even almost raped.
How can he expect us to listen? He has never been
beaten bloody by his father or anyone else.
He has never watched a relative or friend die in agony
or even quietly, yet. (Except his mother long ago and
so slowly.) How can he presume? Why should he stand up
and speak of suffering, or grief? He has never seen anyone
get shot or stabbed in real life. He has never been mugged
or even almost mugged. (The one time he was burglarized,
the event was small and absurd in the tomato-stained
banality of South Philadelphia.) He has never
jumped from a burning house. Did he once survive tornado,
earthquake, flood? Absolutely not. And he sure as hell
never crouched in a fucking jungle ditch while fucking
AK-47 bullets sprayed mud on his fucking helmet.
How does he think he can talk about fear?
He was never tortured by the police of Paraguay
or even arrested in Turkey. He has never spent a single night
in jail. He is practically a stranger to severe pain
(the exceptions were brief) and terrible danger.
He has never tried heroin or even cocaine.
Never did he slit his wrists or even think about it.
In a way the man has barely lived! Yet still

he solicits our attention when we could be listening
to those who have truly suffered. Does he think
everyone has a serious truth? Does he know what modesty is?
Does he think nothing matters but "language"?
Does he regard metaphor as a wardrobe to dress up
triviality? Does he not see
that we couldn't listen to every sad story
even if we wanted to?

Pilgrimage

Those are Hardy cows, I said
wanting to feel something
gazing from Syward Road
across Alington Avenue
where the fields spread calmly
behind red-roofed Dorchester.
Annie and Peter glanced and looked away;
Annie was filing her nails and Peter had a magazine.
So this is it, I thought, as usual
it's just part of the spread of reality
like that roadworker's belly
or that old woman's floppy hat.
Max Gate was closed to the public

but I moved a short way along the drive
and stood one minute to stare at
one brick face of the house
trying to feel the exact air
of Tom and Emma and the great wistfulness;
much seemed gently hid by the screen of leaves.
Hid, hidden, Hardy—

then we drove down to balmy Weymouth
where the public wandered to see what was fun
and pitched pennies at sand sculpture.

On the radio came an invitation to take
a short course in the history of jazz . . .
Annie said something funny and Peter did too;
we took photos on the esplanade;
and crossing the bridge toward the Crown Hotel
we passed a young freckled round-faced woman
whose breasts bounced and bounced and bounced.
(—Arabella!)

Divorce Dream

The marriage was in a last hour of honeycombed decay,
you could tell by the moaning sound of trolleys
and the way memories had gone scaley-thin, one puff of wind
would blow marriage fragments all over the city;
I climbed the dark stairs and sprawled on the sofa,

my wife was extremely not home. The clock was loud
and busy and imperturbable in such dry air.
A phone call to my father seemed a good idea;
seemed necessary; it was the only idea.
I looked around for the phone. Things were different—

because of our being so wrong Annie and I let small things
go awry: the tail of a dead mouse stuck out
from behind a dresser and squirrels played polo
inside the walls so the house trembled
and my stomach too trembled like a dog in its sleep

and our black phone was gone. Then our landlords walked in,
our fat Irish landlords except now they were our tenants
and their children were Chinese and they all spoke
cheerfully about packages of dried noodles and puttered away
in a cloud of happy family. I should call my father—

room to room I walked behind a ribbon of shadow
emitted from a song called "I Don't Wanna Fade Away" . . .
All the lightbulbs were fading; on the carpet
were plops of Thanksgiving gravy; nothing mattered
compared to what mattered. Annie knew this.

Finally in her room I found the phone but it was not black
it was yellow, and it was so complicated, you had to plug it in
three different ways and wind it up and little crucial
knobs and hooks and rings kept falling loose in my hand.

Non-Tenured

The day is HOT. I can feel myself not
getting tenure. To write a book on Frost
or whoever is as far from me as Alaska and I see
me in ten years—not a professor, and
not a lawyer and not an editor making firm decisions
on the twentieth floor in Manhattan. No,

one of those faintly smelly people you meet
occasionally at a party or more oddly
in a restaurant or theater—they recognize you
from somebody's poetry reading, maybe your own—
and suddenly you're up to your neck
in claustrophobic conversation about Rimbaud
with whole stanzas quoted at you in both languages
and those eyes on you with a red burning look
that seems to comment on your prudent success.
Now the subject is Pasternak while the hand shakes a glass,
the drink is spilling and you don't know Pasternak,
how did this start? Those eyes burn
and you sense the job at some banal agency or warehouse
or peculiar local publisher or messenger service,
the elbows of the dark jacket shine unpleasantly,
already you see stacks of manuscript
back in the tilted dustball apartment:

a novel called *Skunkamung Creek* "about the buzzing of flies
in summertime, and a sister who vanishes, and the way
reality decomposes,"
another novel called *Dex Lango's Revenge* "about a detective
being hunted by the robber he once sent to jail, but
really about how language always escapes
the speaker's intention and points toward his death"
and five full-length plays—
the "most polished" is called "Thyroid Rodeo"
while one called "The Bed in the Brain" needs "pruning"—
and incredible pounds of verse:
free verse, "painfully free" but also
an entire fat folder of nothing but villanelles . . .

And now somehow you really are visiting this person:
sidestep jerrybuilt pagodas of piled paperbacks,
Nietzsche catches your eye inevitably
and a history of Hinduism and *Reflections on Violence*;
the portable turntable bears an LP entitled "Jar of Lips"
but Berlioz and Stravinsky lean against one speaker
and apparently
you've agreed to read this person's new thing,
"Ode to Three Animal Lovers" . . . There's a nuance
of rotting spaghetti sauce in the air
as this person hands you a Rolling Rock and utters
a line you'll locate later in "The Witch of Coös,"
handing you the beer and smiling not calmly . . .

Suppose a vastly kind and patient reader were to read
all the works in that apartment—
countless clauses of real force might well be found, unless
the stains on many pages prevented a fair appraisal . . .

You say you have to get home.

                         —Abandoning ME, damn you,
you smug commissar of compromise,
ten years from now—
I'll follow you down to the front door
speaking of Dirck Van Sickle
and I'll grimace at your receding taillights
and baby I'll know something you don't know.

The Halls

Five more books in a box to be carried out to the car;
your office door closes behind you and at that moment
you turn invisible—not even a ghost in that hall
from the hall's point of view.
If the halls don't know you, the halls and the rooms
of the building where you worked for seven years—
if the halls don't know you,

                      and they don't—
some new woman or two new men come clattering
down these halls in the month after your departure, indeed
just two days after you left forever
they come clattering with ideas about
the relation between mind and body or will and fate
filled with hormones of being the chosen workers here
and they feel as if the halls and rooms begin to recognize them,
accept them, as if there is a belonging in the world—

but these new workers are wrong, the halls don't know
who is working under the unobtrusive fluorescent panels;

this is appalling and for a minute you are appalled
though your being so now is not an event
in the life of your new rented house or even
your new condominium . . .
So if they don't, if they don't know you,
the halls, the walls, the fixtures,

then what? Then there is for you
no home in that rock, no home in the mere rock of
where you work, where you briskly walk, not even
in the bed where your body sleeps alone or not—

so if there is to be a place for you, for you
it must not be located in plaster and tile and space,
it will have to be in that other house,
the one whose door you felt opening just last night
when you dialed from memory and your friend picked up the phone.

Pasco, Barbara

I find I am descending in a propeller plane upon Pasco
in the state of Washington. I accept this;
I have reasons for participating in the experiential sequence
that has brought me here. Down below the land is printed
with huge circles, doubtless an irrigation system,
doubtless it makes sense. There are people who understand it
living with dignity in square houses
and the result possibly is one billion radishes.
Now some so-called time has passed. This nation
is a huge nation in which the infinity of for example
Washington State
is just one segment of an even less thinkable hugeness
and yet *zim zim zim zim* United Airlines has me
here in my Eastern metropolis
with its ten thousand makers of third-rate pizza
uncannily far from the possible radishes of Washington State.
The taxi driver experiments with narrow streets
to shorten our detour caused by sports fans and he says
the Eagles will out-tough the Steelers.
I defer to his judgment, I am conserving my powers.
After "a while" I have this unsettlingly smooth tuna salad
with a pale pickle
in a drugstore designed by Dwight D. Eisenhower,
reading a few poems by David Rivard. I have thoughts.

I have my Uncle Ralph's jacket soft and droopy giving me
a Sense of the Past. The rain out there
on the roofs of retail outlets is saying No Guarantee
and in a way I am nowhere, in another way maybe
definitely not. In a wide wet parking lot
I turn back toward the store to explain to the cashier
that she charged me for six cans of seltzer when in fact
I only had one can *from* a six-pack
but the idea of justice seems so fatiguing
I would rather read a surprisingly serious detective novel
so I vibrate with indecision in the parking lot
till all the car windows rattle imperceptibly. Then
an alleged interval ostensibly intervenes, at the mall
a woman at a piano has played 1800 songs from memory
according to the radio personality who stands with a mike
explaining her bid for the Guinness Book of Records.
I am walking away at an unplanned angle singing "Tiny Montgomery"
which I bet she wouldn't have been ready to play.
I have this inner life, I think of my father
lonely in Vermont, I think of myself lonely in Syracuse
and my old poem about a detective who can't solve his biggest case
and as a result I have feelings—but my teacher said
the future of American poetry can't be merely
the notation of sensibility. When he said that I felt
a chilly fear at the edge of consc-consc-consc-consciousness
like an ice cube in the corner of my stomach.
That's how I felt. So then, so then consequently
I thought "I must gather up some serious ideas" but then
Ashbery phoned and left a message after the beep,
"Don't be a sucker, ideas are where it *isn't*."
This made my throat get sort of dry so I drank a Classic Coke
and then another Classic Coke two hours later
as time so-to-say passed. What was always there?
Texture, that's what, how it was/is, the how of how;

when I pick up my color prints at the camera shop
the disappointment I always feel is actually a blessing
is it not? I can say "I'll go along with this charade
until I can think my way out" even though I'll never
think my way out. I've come this far;
that day in 1971 I hitchhiked all the way to Montpelier
didn't I? And here I am.
Suddenly I have a son
who focuses with tremendous insistence upon
dogs, balloons, air conditioners, hats, clocks, and noses.
To him I convey that the world is okay:
life is good: we accept it. Your dad is a little mixed up
but your shoes got tied, right?
As Barbara Cohen in high school said about politics
it's interesting, giving the word four earnest syllables,
in-ter-est-ing.

Removal Service Request

It is 2:45 A.M. I can't sleep. This apartment is too noisy.
It's totally quiet. It's filled with the noise of the past.
How does anyone sleep after the age of thirty-five? Things
gather in your apartment and stay, each thing learns
to emit its own signal, its own night-noise;
you bring them to your next apartment and each thing gives
its offended cry—your eyes open in the dark.
There should be a service a person could call
to get some relief . . .

Crystal Clearance Experts,
Stark & Stark Divestment Consultants,
pragmatic seraphim from a god of gentle oblivion:
Take away the heartbreaking photographs!
You with your white pickup truck whose bumper says
DUMP IT OR LUMP IT
you should come now and take away
the heartbreaking photographs:
take the odd and ill-focused and ostensibly forgettable
along with the obviously poignant—they're all
too restless tonight, keening in their swollen albums—

empty the closet:
there is a pale blue suit that knows too much about
vows not kept
and thirty shirts hang there nursing thirty claims:

one from I know who in Syracuse,
seven from someone who did love me in Connecticut,
and the strange papery shirt that once belonged to
Morgan who loved Ada in a story that would mean nothing almost
except Jessica was in it and I loved her;
and the decent un-suave green shirt
chosen by my mother twenty-four years ago,
it still fits.
Take them. And from the linen shelf take
the blue flowered pillowcase
that still knows what it knows of sleepers sleeping in 1978.
Leave that shelf bare: subtract:
leave me standing alone under one naked burning bulb
a freed man—

take the books:
remove a novel given by its lonesome author I never read
and *The Icon and the Axe*, which I never read with Cathy,
and two books I carried on lunch breaks in the summer of '81
because they won't shut up about the self I intended;
take the book I read on a plane to San Francisco
trying to build a *rich inner life* before I knew it would become
this rain forest of murmurs and calls all night.
The bookcases are roped with vines, thick
unchoppable vines of memory
come chop them now! It is 2:49 A.M.—
this apartment is all vines, all noise of vines
I've had it! Seraphim,
fleet removers with transparent gloves come now:

don't fail to seize the videotape
of a four-year-old boy maneuvering toy trains and helicopters
in the gray-tiled corridor of this apartment
this apartment not his home though he was my son—and is—

removers: get it all:
cart off all cherishability.
I just remembered my box of 45s—it chatters now unbearably;
I know who sat half-happily on a fold-out bed in Watertown
agreeing that the Chiffons and the Dixie Cups were so fine;
nail shut that box and pitch it
from the stern of a fast black ship

because: I cannot be Mister Elegy all night!
To be Mister Elegy all night is a busy kind of death.
I need a sleep in which the past is not Times Square.
O lord of silence, Chief of Unloading Unlimited
send viewless unprecedented nymphs
who'll kidnap me to a vast white casino
where the only books in my suite are science fiction
and orgasm comes every hour
with a new steak-fed cheerleader who majors in chemistry
and says "Oh, incredible" . . .

Or not.
        Or not. I'm tired. Those cheerleaders—
I see them turning on the TV in my priceless suite
to watch some game show I never heard of,
I see their skin 21 smooth 21 smooth 21 smooth
till I'm all too safe and blank to get an erection
or just too human anyway I'm tired, tired enough to sleep now;
removers, return,
infiltrate the white casino and take me home.

Tonette

I said yes to Tish and Pat
in Mrs. Conmack's fourth grade when they asked
if I'd be in a tonette trio with them
to play "Down in the Valley" and "Working on the Railroad"
in front of the class—though I must have known
it was risky I said yes because—
because life was so rich, so startling and so *involved*
with the frightening beauty of the smiles of girls,
and to say no seemed a terrible shrinking
from the challenge of the glory of life.
I said yes to Tish and Pat and they smiled;

but I did not practice at home.
What did I imagine would happen? It seems
I felt the beauty of the girls and the courage of my *yes*
would be enough, and my reward for just being there
and standing up in front of the whole class
amid the deluge of life's stunning overstimulation
would be a magical rightness of fingering
when I gripped the stubby black tonette and blew.
I did not practice at home. There was my arithmetic to do
and the Geography chapter about llamas and Peru,
there was important cowboy action on TV—

surely I must have rehearsed once with Tish and Pat?
But if so, I joked my way through it,
and I suspect they supported my notion that girls
needed to practice tonette whereas a boy
who got A's in arithmetic and must some day inherit
the world's beauty would just naturally know
every note to hit. But I didn't, oh Lord:
all I could play was the first five or six notes
of each song and then confusion flooded me,
I was whelmed and lost in the gorgeous alien world—

Tish and Pat played on, playing carefully
to make up for the red-faced boy who stood beside them
in front of the vast fourth-grade class
and Mrs. Conmack who saw everything
and I kept twisting the mouthpiece of my black tonette,
all through the one hundred hours of Tish and Pat
playing every note of each enormous melody
I twisted that mouthpiece and made faces to indicate
that if only my instrument were properly aligned
I could play "Down in the Valley" all day—

nobody believed that bit of theater for a second.
Not for a second. When the epic performance ended
I went to my seat grinning with ears like scarlet beacons,
my grin tried to say "Boys don't need music"
but said instead "I am lost on this planet."
Mrs. Conmack let it pass and called on the next performers
and I sat not quite knowing that I would never forget.

Yes is fine; but don't fake your tonette.

Self-Importance

Last night when I washed the dishes every move I made
had a heroic kind of distinction. Do these two forks at once,
rinse them swiftly, drop them in the drainer deftly
producing that satisfactory clatter, now do the plates,
washing the bottoms as well as the tops, my left hand
so acrobatic in its connubial cooperation with my right—
where is Martin Scorsese, doesn't he want to get this
on film? Me—
washing those dishes last night, and
today on this airplane:
I am the great adventure.
The flight attendant's voice explains
that in the unlikely event of a water landing
my seat cushion can be used as a flotation device.
Water landing is a funny euphemism but I don't feel sarcastic,
I feel respectful of the entire flight crew, because
they have roles to play in extending the adventure of me.
A number of the other passengers look like
people who should not die prematurely, they look
important to someone in some sphere of activity.
That's nice; but it is small potatoes. Whereas
I am in this largeness located right here above my neck.
There are ten or even twenty people who would care a lot
if I crashed to the bottom of the sea but besides that
there is this more palpable kind of importance:
it bubbles in me.

It's not about being perfect—
admittedly I say stupidly vague things many times per day.
I can just barely do the simplest task with a screwdriver.
Admittedly there is a relation between
my sense of ambiguity everywhere and the possibility of
moral cowardice concealed in my soul. Admittedly
I made my ex-wife sad so that I could be more happy.
So I'm not the greatest guy. That's not the point.
Somebody out there could call me "average"
and articulate a perspective from which what happens to me
is small potatoes; that's pretty funny because
in the basic sense what happens to me is *the* great potato
at the center of the earth.

I don't know why

I am such big news. It gets scary not knowing why—
I wish the world would tell me why!
Not telling me is damned ungracious of the world
when it is so obviously counting on me to make it matter.
Being me involves presidential levels of stress.
If someone embarrasses me by showing in conversation
that I have faked some knowledge of nineteenth-century British history
this turns out to be a calamity requiring hours of
brooding. As I get dressed the next morning
I pause between buttons *and* between shoes
to relive the embarrassment, each second of it on video replay
like a dropped pass in the fourth quarter at the Rose Bowl.
How did the ambush develop, how to protect the presidential self
from bitter incursions of the "truth" of others? Because

the profound animal that looks out from my eyes
has this ADVENTURE to enact which is me.

If I don't do it

there will be this empty hole this gaping huge hole
at the middle of the world—
canyon of air, vacancy at the White House,
sheer pit of space—

if I were not zealous
in SUStaining and EXtending the big news of
every little thing that happens to me
not to mention big things that should happen to me,
me get great job
me get manifested admiration of intense vigorous women
me march onward toward such victories
inch closer foot closer great leap closer
the adventure goes on all day *every day*!—
Amazing that I don't collapse,
awesomely heroic that I ride and ride
via varied modes of transportation
accepting this bizz buzz bizz buzz in my head always
for the sake of the world's heart-pulsing core-adventure
to which everything pertains—

every story that has a hero, of course,
and the safe landing of certain significant planes.

Soul on Bench

"Call the world if you Please 'The vale of Soul-making'
Then you will find out the use of the world . . .
Do you not see how necessary a World of Pains and
troubles is to school an Intelligence and make it a soul?"

—Keats in a letter of April 1819

If it is a vale of soul-making
then the fact that I just missed my train
is merely incidental. The point is
how I respond. I tipped the cabdriver
as much as usual—not his fault
the streets were flooded by all-night rain—
and I helped a woman with her vast suitcase.
That suitcase should have been on wheels.
And I should be on a train right now
but that's not the point. There is
bigger business at issue here: the making
of a soul. Which is why on this bench
I sit so philosophically. My wrist is sore
from the weight of that unlikely suitcase

but this minor pain is a kind of food
for my soul in its long slow brood.
There is a rhyming of pain
with rain and train and in my soul
these words fall into place
in a comforting iambic way, rhyming also with plane
because having missed the god-damned train
I will probably also miss my plane
and my entire weekend might be screwed—
but it's a kind of food
in the long slow stomach of my soul.
Dignity, and not Detroit, must be my goal
and that's why I'm so calm on this bench
regardless of Fortune's incidental deals
and how (for example) my wrist feels.
But that suitcase should have been on wheels.

Fear of Concrete

What if the blocks of compressed pulverized
the blocks of con- con- concrete
of ten trillion infinitesimal
What if those big slabs those slabs and the cost
the metal-stress analysis the cost overruns
and the vectors, the charts
indicating shipments of power-cut sheared blocks
and how many for each wall, those walls lit by
municipal electric all night in winter wind
that reality: slabs; graphs and copper pipes
plug fuse voltage meter ratchet ratio dredge winch
ten-inch bolts—
if that reality were to refuse limitation?
If all that were to reject co-presence with

    this other inner other this
    swirling adoration of nuance this love:
    what we feel what say what we say we feel
    what I feel you say what we might mean
    what Coleridge may what Hopkins
    what about Blake not straight solid sense
    the not measurable love loving the names Rilke
    Dickinson what we could mean Baudelaire
    Yeats and Stevens both in the air
    Chrissie Hynde and *heart* and *dream* and *seem*—

Some nights I see that BOLT REALITY brunking outward
in blocks all through all, crunking in blitz vehicles
in all directions on mashed mud: so that then
I couldn't keep on just rubbing my cheek cool
along the smoothness of right phrases
but that then the blocks would load my hands
the drills would shriek all day flicking hail
of pulverized dredged byproduct over my hair
coating my brow making heavy my coat
all clogged in petrifaction for listed purposes
on a winter winter day. That that.
Plexi-fiber-laser-solder-nitro-chunkizing: target triangulation.
Huge coils of black wire, computerized rationing of food,
officers shaking their heads canceled canceled canceled
under block-shadow the dwarves of production shiver
to receive paycheck take a number stand in line—
down to what it comes down to at base at the base:

poetry gone, me moused, the no-joke blocks piled clear to heaven.

Ballad of Little Millard

Little Millard flexed in his black suit because
he smelled some blueberry cobbler just a month ahead.
For him for him for him but Mrs. Schmitz had other ideas
as did Mr. Skib and they mailed him to the canyon
of copper wire in the valley of metal where he stacked
J-valves and interstitial hasp-flanges on dollies
and swung them onto freight lifts coated with decades
of obscene hints. What about me cried Millard
during the gray coffee and cloudbursts of iron shavings
gave sole answer. His cot was a tongue depressor.
His mirror was a loud joke in Spanish downstairs.
Slate was the cold water, ice was the can opener,
sugar were the gossip columns on the cracking tiles;
months were sodden boxes ditched behind Salvation Army.
Every day there was defecation, spud peels and dead mouse.
Little Millard cramped up in his black suit.
It's not funny, his best friend would have said
if he'd had a friend at all at all. Later
little Millard would die, access-haunted still because
even in the canyon of copper wire in the valley of metal

there was an hour of the scent of Veronica Tingle
terribly like blueberry pie and even a minute
that seemed in memory to have included huge lips
and there was the long whistle of a train not a freight
rushing through the valley to the *next* valley—

Thrall

All the wanting and not having oilspills my room
and darkens the thickened air.
If I could forget—
but young women of venturesome litheness
and moderately priced unpretentiously good ethnic restaurants
force me to care.

Timberwolf

So, you are feeling ironical about my sentimentality?
Well I feel ironical about that. This kid may be small
but he sure isn't fat. You start using the word "romantic"
as a blowtorch I can leave the building. You won't miss me?
Fine. I can go to San Francisco, or maybe baby go
to some nonvicious milieu in the Midwest. Pluralism
cuts both ways, what? Goodbye, thanks for the chat.
Pat, this game isn't over yet! That's right, Tony,

and this man plays ball right down to the final second
regardless of the scoreboard and Tony, you can't ask
for more than that. That's right, Pat. It has not been
a precision type of game—let's get a word with Sedale
during this timeout. We made some mistakes but
we kept on coming. Thanks, Sedale. Mistakes, Tony,
they come with the territory

but this young man sits up very late with strong dark tea
bombarded by photographs that keep announcing
in shiny voices *This is over* while the carpet is
obviously dirty as the carpet was in Providence
twenty-two years back and the clock needs oil
and so not to let it all make terrible sense takes
a type of resistance. Okay, he's not young, he was
but now he's not, Pat. The pile of cassettes topples over.
It has not been a precision type of game. But Tony,

if he is 45 it is a twisty 45, though he loves the semicolons
because they show respect he knows you don't want to get caught
staring at those big electric numbers and he can cope
with the commas, so many commas, are you saying
a big hero then? No, not that, Pat, but this guy
is living minute by minute; he concedes nothing
that's right Tony. You might say self-absorbed
like a character in Ann Beattie someone might say but

oh, but oh when he squints in fluorescent 2 A.M.
it's to slide past the grapple of what would be too plain
for all of us, Pat, for every player in the league;
admittedly the word "slide" he has used too often
but as an ex-almost-priest said to me more than once
we do what we can. It's to live *in*
the perpetual heart-smirch and heart-slice without
just tanking and without denying that it *is* heart-life
including indeed heartbreak. Well, but
you haven't earned that word "heartbreak"
oh haven't I? Who said I was through?
Clock's tickin' dude. This man is only 46, Tony,
and when his plane touches down in San Francisco
he grabs his Timberwolves tote bag so firmly.
And here outside our studio there's an old man
riding a brown bicycle past Verna Funeral Parlor
and the big radio tied to the handlebars is playing
"Duke of Earl."

II

Loaded Inflections

It's a good thing there is posterity—
or it's a good thing there is God—
because otherwise—
we'd be in just this cold soup, this cold mulligatawny
of everybody's skewed opinions. At lunch

Brian praises Geffle's new book and I say "Well, but
it all seems so humorless" and a little later
I praise Conkley's recent book and Brian says "Maybe
but the poems seem so cozy, so pleased to whip up
the same yelp of the Tortured Spirit, over and over."

Next day having coffee with Eric
I rather recklessly praise some of Prinshod's poems
and Eric says "If only he wasn't always
mounting his bardic steed"
and we both laugh at how apt this criticism indeed is.
Outside the Honeydew, a young woman in a dark raincoat
with long red hair and a red bookbag glances in at us
or at others near us as if wondering whether we might be
seriously interesting. She moves out of sight.
A truck bearing the name of a potato chip company
makes an assertive turn and clunks out of sight in the rain.
Eric mentions the poems of L. B. Smegg
and I quote Brian saying "They *look* like poems"
and the loaded inflection is cause for more laughter—
happy laughter—

                    although
we're not stupid enough not to know
that in another cafe in Boston or Madison or New Haven
or Ann Arbor or Baltimore or Houston
or Iowa City or Manhattan or Berkeley
someone who has published three "well-received" books
is commenting very briefly
on my new book, or on Eric's, saying of Eric
"he pretends to know much more than he knows" or
"he never sounds like a real person" or saying of me
"Halliday thinks his most banal experiences are poetry already"
or "he has no *ear*" or

whatever. Eric and I are smart enough
to almost hear that conversation, at a distance,
through the rain outside the Honeydew,
and we try to season, to temper our judgments,
to reflect—

but only God, or the genius critic of the next century,
truly hears all of both conversations, ours today plus
the one about us in Princeton or Denver or Chapel Hill
and all those others
down here on the North American continent
where it is raining in some cities and sunny in others,
God or that critic hearing not only our inflections
but everything we don't quite say that loads them up;
and there is a patient reckoning
when all the voices have stopped.
That's when the true red meat gets separated from
the potato chips—and the living metaphors from
the ones that are stinking dead
or just pathetic . . .

God, god,
lucky for us that we know God is there—
on the job, above the soup—
God or the great deep persons of 2045—

since if we didn't know this
we might buy into cheap effects, little splashes,
hit-and-run raids, in-crowd alliances
like kids on a rainy playground spending recess
till a bell that never rings.

Poetry Friendship on Earth

He thinks I'm pretty good—a lot of the time . . .
But he has reservations. Something about my "looseness,"
something about "a tang of narcissism" . . . And he is
my friend! My trusted friend. I mean he and I go back,
we must have had fifty lunches, since 1979
we must have sent each other sixty really good funny letters
about poetry, our stuff, other people's stuff; we've had
an understanding . . . So why can't he think my poems are
perfect? I don't mean perfect but
I mean like terrifically good with that certain radiance,
that *glow* I see emitted by the pages of my manuscript.
He of all people should see it. God knows
I've done my best to see and praise what's good
in his work—despite his tendency toward the unsayable phrase
and his habit of giving poem after poem the same pattern or shape.
Does he realize, I wonder, that I do have reservations
about his work? If he does it's because I've been honest
and he ought to be grateful for that. He ought to see
how my honesty is profoundly involved in the originality and
freshness of my work. He's very smart but somehow
he never *quite* seems to catch on, to wake up
to how special my talent is. But

it's okay, I can wait;

maybe he's just distracted—he's been so busy lately. Really
he's a fine person with a fine mind. Basically he's a great guy.

I'll send him my new poem and this time maybe he'll shed
that crust of slightly cranky differentness that has slightly
clogged conversation during some of our fifty lunches
and this time maybe he'll feel the way the words *had* to come out
exactly the way they did for me
and he'll say "I wouldn't change a syllable," he'll say
"Jesus, Mark, this is *it*! I only wish *I'd* written it."

Legs

In the last year of my marriage,
among a hundred other symptoms I wrote a poem called
"The Woman across the Shaft"—she was someone
I never met—she had long bare legs
on a summer night when she answered the phone
in her kitchen and lifted her legs to the table
while she talked and laughed and I tried to listen
from my window across an airshaft between buildings
and watched her legs. I doubt she was beautiful
but her legs were young and long
and she laughed on the phone

while I sat in my dark of dissolving faith

and I tried to capture or contain the unknown woman
in a poem: the real and the ideal,
the mess of frayed bonds versus untouched possibility,
so forth. Embarrassed now
I imagine a female editor
who received "The Woman across the Shaft"
as a submission to her magazine—the distaste she felt—
perhaps disgust she felt—I imagine her
grimacing slightly as she considers writing "Pathetic"
on the rejection slip but instead lets the slip stay blank
and then turns to another envelope
from a writer she has learned to trust,
crossing her long legs on her smart literary desk.

The Ivory Novel

It occurs to me now that I could write a novel
about the Fate of the Elephant,
the illegal hunting of elephants in Africa—
I feel now how I could do this:
a thick strong solid novel of bitter realism:

there would be the young naive journalist
who slowly catches on to the obscenity of the hunting,
and there would be the cynical older man,
an embassy official maybe or wildlife photographer
who somehow finds himself beginning to care
until by page 200 he cares desperately;
maybe because of a certain woman
who loves animals . . . Through her eyes he can see
the great sweet nobility of the lumbering elephants
and when he comes upon the hacked gray corpses
in their lakes of dried mammal blood he feels
the quickening of rage that makes him younger
but also, of course, more vulnerable. Thus
it will be the young journalist who ends up stronger
though at the same time hardened, divested
of the charming illusions that made him so funny
in the first hundred pages. And he's the one
who finally gets the girl, or woman, whatever—
unless there'd be two women, yes, a sultry brunette
and this younger very slim one—lots of possibilities—

so, three or four characters on the good side
versus the foul poachers, swarthy types soaked with sweat,
and the greedy ivory dealer who owns five airplanes
and bribes the police (of Kenya, Uganda, Congo)
and ultimately arranges the murder of one protagonist
in the teeming marketplace of Bujumbura
because he or she knows too much, but meanwhile
the dealer is actually subtly unhappy and one long night
he reveals this to the woman from the Park Service
in a dialogue that deepens my novel considerably.
Also: huge heaps of local color, the wind on the veldt,
the herds wandering on immemorial paths, the humorless lions
watching from the tall grass, and red dust billowing
from the wheels of bouncing Jeeps. All this,

320 pages. I could do this. Presumably I would need,
in addition to research, a trip to Kenya for three weeks
to pick up details for that texture of authenticity;
this investment would pay off. Because
I can see how my book would be a hit. I can see an ad
that says "SHATTERING" and "INCREDIBLY MOVING"
and a review that mentions not only Peter Matthiessen
but also Conrad as my sort-of equals. I can see
the glossy jacket—it gives me a thrill of deathlessness:
Fellow Creatures. I see myself
in years thereafter feeling—at times—
that I have actually helped save the African elephant
from extinction.
                    Would that be true?

I guess not. Possibly? But I think not.
Undoubtedly I could help the elephant in more direct ways
if I wanted to . . .

                    My novel, though "MOVING,"
has a tragic darkness that tends to discourage activism.
For instance, in Chapter Twelve we find
that one of the foul poachers is not really foul at all
but a man with five children, a father who believes
that without the work of his heavy rifle
his sickly daughters would die. Mubende carries photos of them
in the leather case that holds his long gray bullets.
Literary art! Art! Art eternal; and mild
elephants with shattered brains . . .
I am not going to write the elephant novel;

but I guess I'll write poems in some ways not different.

Novelists of 2007

The novelists of 2007 will reach back and back, trying
to capture 1991. They will hunch at their computers,
wearing the goggles that will have become standard equipment,
peering at the dark gray measured spaces between yellow words
to see the poorly lit rooms of 1991; who
is there on the sofa? Who
is calling from that narrow kitchen with the brick-tile walls?

Tired loyal earnest novelists, wanting not to fake it,
scanning their inner screens for true blips of what was:
they will see the rooms of 1991 in mesmerizing subliminal flashes
as if from windows of a speeding train and their heads will ache
with the effort to make that train slow down.
In the end they will mostly settle for
accuracies of street names, brand names, news—
black clouds over Kuwait on TV, some fairly true claim
about clothing styles in 1991 (so easily confused
with those of '92) and how we still imagined
we could safely stay on the beach all day in July,
and jokes about Dan Quayle (not Gerald Ford) . . .
But when the novelists give up and go to bed in 2007
they'll still feel (the honest ones) that the truth
of '91, its life blood, has not been saved on their disks;

they'll sense the escape of Donna's exact type of laugh
when Gabriella fed herself yogurt for the first time
and how the yellow roses leaned when Jill put them
in the Ninja Turtles mug while Nick sang "Sad Sad Sad"
in a space thatched with the unmade movies of lived life
and how they themselves (the novelists) felt good and bad
about being only twenty-five with all their astounding work ahead
and how the dialogue when your two tangled friends nearly broke up
was not efficient and crisply dramatic but still held
fear-and-love swirled over fear-and-love
like the water of four rivers that come to fill
a storm-rippled lake.
That's the book they'll read before they wake.

Alley Sketch

Filling the small yards of the alley behind my house
there is the gray light of eight o'clock
on a Saturday morning, the kind of light
that makes you want to utter words
like "gray" and "wash" and "drift"
and to speak of innocence and quiet potential
as if many beautiful real things were willing to occur
in time, later, simply when the day is ready.
Small unassuming birds of several species
are busily accepting the available
in the gray light of the alley's back yards
and the stout Greek woman across from here
is mildly shaking something out her window.
—Are you getting the picture?
And the feeling of the picture?
But suppose I were a better writer, suppose I gave you now
ten more lines describing the alley and its light,
evoking the paradoxical beauty of drabness,
the gentle obscure suspension of eight o'clock
in which taxation and disease are not denied
but so calmly and pervasively postponed . . .
What would we have?

Or suppose then I made up a word that would mean
precisely this hour's light:

draevelmo—
how good would this be?
Then there would be this useful term
by which any speaker of English could immediately
summon up just this alley world where the brown dog
noses at a rusting trash can
and feels no need, for the present, to bark.
Then we could bypass the imagery, the old piecework
of lyrical evocation,
those never-quite-right approximations that keep us
somewhere not quite at home with the, the
innocence, the utter patience of Saturday morning
that can easily wait lifetimes for us to get
even slightly, even faintly closer to
draevelmo . . .
We'd be there!—Or at least,
we could say so perfectly where we weren't.

The Scene

Thank you for the compliment. I will assume
it is partly sincere. And soon, when I compliment
your work, I will try hard to be sincere.
Thus our relations will be cordial—thus we may be grateful
for the social scene that prompts from us these compliments.
But what I want—
                    ten or eleven years from now
you stand at a window, early on a winter morning;
it is a week or a month after the death of
someone you knew well; you gaze out upon the chill stiff scene
of trees and stone walls, gray and black and gray . . .
Admire my work then. Love it then.

Threads

Whether or not they moved into a blue clapboard duplex
in their mid-thirties, Ted and Tina—
clapboard?—bringing three bicycles
and the case of Beaujolais given them years before
by Uncle James who said, as if he knew what was to come,
"This will refine your thoughts" and
five mirrors and five small boxes of old letters
(Ted: three; Tina: two), Tina insisting
the sand-colored carpet must be professionally cleaned
at a cost which Ted called "really absurd";
and whether as a result of the new location
Tina met a young Irish theorist at the Dorrwar Bookshop
who introduced her and Ted to the artist Ted would call
the Rembrandt of the Eighties whose talk apparently
precipitated Tina's essay "Eidolons and the Muser's Eye"
it seems certain that in that period one action pointed
to another
otherwise
Ted's friend Alberto two years later might not have written
what he wrote about his mother (the painter) dying including
the beautiful "sand between our toes" passage
which Ted more than once read aloud in the International House
of Pancakes to among others R. Glenn Paul the budding
Spenser scholar who pined for Tina till 1990 swearing
only she enabled him to *see*
and Jayne Alice Orson the imminent star of the purple movie

"Ardalion and Lydia" which won a small obsessive audience
for director Lona Moseley throughout the decade and caused
both Ted and Alberto's brother Juan the accordionist
to lie sleepless many nights or ride bicycles till dawn—
a web of truth stretches among these facts surely
and if this web does not shine importantly
then everything is too sad; hence our research.
Some sources say it was in fact at Café Budapest
that Ted recited Alberto's page about the shadows at midnight
in Memorial Hospital and the waitress allegedly proposed
to marry him (Ted? or Alberto?) on the spot. There was
an intensity, an atmosphere in which each minute counted,
almost a chemical glow around their heads . . .
Why did Tina leave Ted? This we can't know
till the green box is opened, but the web already shines for us
under the moonlike light of inquiry, as we note for instance
that when Ted joined the Garcia group late in '87
young Lloyd Zebrun had not yet departed and was just on
"the maddening edge" of composing the end of
    That Lingering Smoke.

Festbroch's Treichmord

Vaglan Festbroch wrote the Treichmord Symphony
in which the prioletti strings express
his memories of the heron flocks on the Blenen River
in the final summer before Charsk and his Bronze Draloons
defeated the Toff of Molkling and instituted changes
which led to the damming of the Blenen at Karsono.
It was Festbroch who wrote the symphony.
Not someone else. If it had been someone else,
we would be uttering a name other than Vaglan Festbroch
if the Treichmord were still the symphony that it is.
Our experience of recalling the Treichmord
so as to speak of it in comparison with other experiences
would be different to the extent that the name
Vaglan Festbroch
does create a difference; and our lives would be
different then—
                        but we must live the life given,
as we can, and in this world it is Festbroch
who gathers unto his name our sense of poignancy
in the vanishing of those delicate herons of the Blenen.
In some other world another composer named, say, Jort Kyoshlin
might have given us, via prioletti strings,
a vision of herons more grand or purple, or of
snowy geese. But would that have been the Treichmord?

There cannot be two!
Ourselves not having been Kyoshlin,
our fate in this has been Festbroch

and Festbroch must be enough;
his Treichmord our only Treichmord before the infinite silence.

III

Bad People

The guys who drank quarts of Busch last night
here by the backstop of this baseball diamond
had names given them by their mothers and fathers—
"Jack" and "Kenny" let us say.

Jack might be
a skinny guy in a black fake-leather jacket,
he's twenty-five, his gray pants are too loose on his hips,
his jaws always have these little black extra hairs,
his mother won't talk to him on the phone,
she lives on french fries and ketchup,
he hasn't been able to send her any cash
in the last two years, ever since he lost
the job unloading produce trucks at Pathmark;
Jack's father disappeared when he was ten.
"No big deal," Jack says, "he was a bastard anyway,
he used to flatten beer cans on the top of my head."
Kenny offers a laugh-noise. He's heard all that before.
Kenny is forty-eight, a flabby man with reddened skin,
he is employed at the Italian Market selling fish
just four hours a day but his shirts hold the smell;
his female companion Deena left him a note last month:
"You owe me $12 chocolate $31 wine $55 cable TV plus
donuts—I have had it—taking lamp and mirror
they are mine." Kenny hasn't seen her since.
He hangs with Jack because Jack talks loud

as if the world of cops and people with full-time jobs
could be kept at bay by talking, talking loud . . .

(I'm talking gently and *imaginatively* here
as if the world of bums and jerks could be kept far off—)

Jack and Kenny. (Or two other guys dark to me with wounds
oozing in Philadelphia ways less ready to narrate.)
Last night at midnight they got cheesesteaks at Casseloni's
and bought four quarts at the Fireside Tavern
and wandered into this park. After one quart of Busch
Jack said he was Lenny Dykstra
and found a stick for his bat. "Pitch to me asshole" he said
so Kenny went to the mound and pitched his bottle
for want of anything better and Jack swung in the dark and missed;
Kenny's bottle smashed on home plate and Jack heard in the sound
the absurdity of all his desiring since seventh grade,
absurdity of a skinny guy who blew everything since seventh
when he hit home runs and chased Joan Rundle around the gym
so Jack took his own empty bottle and smashed it down
amid the brown shards of Kenny's bottle.
Then they leaned on the backstop to drink the other two quarts
and they both grew glum and silent
and when they smashed these bottles it was like
what else would they do? Next morning

Nick and I come to the park with a rubber ball
and a miniature bat. Nick is not quite three
but he knows the names of all the Phillies starters
and he knows the area around home plate is not supposed to be
covered with jagged pieces of brown glass. Like a good dad
I warn him not to touch it and we decide to establish
a new home plate closer to the mound (there's no trash can
handy). "Who put that glass there?" Nick wants to know
and to make a long story short I say "Bad people."
Nick says "Bad? How come?"

Eighth Avenue Incident

Crossing Eighth Avenue amid shoppers on Christmas Eve
I saw an attractive young white woman
crossing the other way with several packages and bags.
She looked anxious, and I felt
a flash of sadness that I could not comfort her
and that I could not make her Christmas smooth
and that I would never see her again
and that love does not save us from tensions and burdens
but indeed love pushes us across the crowded city
encumbered and hastening through the chilly dusk,
the dusky chill . . . And feeling this complicated
flash of sadness I turned while still moving
to glance back at the attractive young white woman
and wish her silently a happy Christmas.
As a result I bashed into a middle-aged black woman
hard enough to knock her backward a pace
(I caught her hip with my canvas suitcase).
"Excuse me! Sorry!" I exclaimed
with an extra verve because it was Christmas Eve.
She just gave me a look
that seemed to mean "Get serious" rather than "Go to hell"
and continued on her way
in the same direction as the other woman, the one
who'd caught my eye without feeling my force.

Cleveland

In Cleveland there is a single mother named Janey
waiting for a bus, trying to concentrate
on a science-fiction novel in the muddle of late afternoon.
She glances far up the avenue—no bus.
Late afternoon in Cleveland.
She has a six-year-old son named Harold.
Janey is twenty-seven, almost twenty-eight.
This bus tends to run a little late.

In Philadelphia I sit feeling obscure
in just the regular way and I think of
the surplus of human poignancy out there
and this image of Janey comes up
and the sensation is not of inventing but of respecting
what's there. In Cleveland there.

Three young men with a basketball pass Janey on the sidewalk
and she notices (without seeming to notice)
that all three of them give her a second look.
In her gaze there is something stern
as she watches for the bus far up the avenue;
she feels the three men are part of reality
and she has become increasingly realistic in Cleveland
where you have to choose which reality to deal with when.
A few years ago, Janey thinks, I would have had
three looks from each guy. That was then:
she was a three-look problem for men.

Momentary nostalgia for being just very pretty.
Harold's after-school program closes at five-thirty.
Janey frowns at her novel about a world not dirty;
it's quite intelligent; it's by Sheri S. Tepper.
Harold's going to want pizza for supper.

—All right,
                                    my respectful interest in Janey is suspect;
indeed it is obviously not untainted by sexual sentimentality.
Watching those three basketball guys recede Janey feels
they are roughly as important as a writer in some other metropolis
who might be imagining her right now
for purposes of sexual sentimentality.

Scraps of the *Plain Dealer* and specks of grit
travel briefly in the urban breeze—
the bus arrives with a business of brakes and gears.
Cleveland,
late afternoon.
Long days make years. She has two tickets to see the Cavaliers.
Taking her poignancy with her like a fabulous tale
I haven't read, Janey gets on her bus and disappears.

Skirt

The very fact that her skirt swirls
bespeaks something that compels my interest
as if not because the skirt covers her ass and thighs
as if I mean not only because given a chance I'd want
very very much probably to help her take the skirt off
in a fantasy bedroom, but for some more lovely reason
more lovely I mean because more mysterious
when she swirls my head turns on my not-merely-biological neck
to follow the play of shadow in those folds of cloth—

in the swirling there is some meaning that draws me
without specific reference I'm saying to her vagina
somewhere beneath the skirt and what my penis might get to do;

it's about a flowing quality in life I'm serious
about something flowing like light among branches
on a windy day, the truth or a truth of how
the beauty of our life is like a winding river
under rapid shifting clouds and how the river is change
and change is possibility and our infinity of possibility is
what makes us not just banal dogs wagged by our tails.
There across the crowded room she turns and turns,
her hair swings, her skirt swirls, she doesn't know
I'm standing here with these deep insights into everything

but if I write it all down with a lovely
swirling of its own she might read it and see
that if I stare at her it is not just the usual but
because I am *interesting* here alone at the edge of the dance.

Sci-fi Floater Genius

I know it's all not real
and I know this with a knowledge like steel
which is to say unbreakable which is why
I can ride their illusory vehicles
east to west over their meticulously fabricated townscape
smiling to myself down the Silver Sabre River
which is in my head.

That's not something I have to explain
that is something they cannot detain
it is a private river of not exactly water
of which the formula is secret but silicon is one aspect
and platinum is one aspect but I reveal no more.
Did you think transit would be simple
between nonreality and ultrareality?
The jingling comes back it must be a warning
I must interrupt transmission

. . . but all this out there is not real
and that is the key. Once I knew that,
I became safe beyond damage zone;
smiling with my lips lifted back from my teeth
down the Silver Sabre River to my base
at Station Momazz. Do not ask about Momazz.
—And I am so safe

except when some things—
shrapnel mirage stimuli—
Laurinda with the long hips
Becky with the exaggerating boobs
NOTHING
Sophie with that unexpected firmness
Tracy of wet lips
they would have fragged me into jittering red steak chunks
if I didn't know the truth and the river

ever cool ever cool ever cool
I *am* sitting still
down my river not to explain they cannot detain
ever cool NO PROBLEM: them
and the "men" they think are smart those androids of gesture
they are Difficulty Level Zero as soon as I just know
how it's *all* only tease-flick light shows
my jingling head caught in transient hoax brainstorm
till I get fine again to feel
with this knowledge like blue steel
how it's all not real
and raft away grinning on the river in my head.

Partial Relief

Sharon running like a pony across the Carolina yard.
Abbie having to tell her son she'll die, "It does seem hard."

David recalling his brother's funny song about crawfish.
At a window above Pine Street, someone's midnight wish.

The poignancy of the human is nearly too much to stand.
The way a small child at a street-corner takes your hand.

From ache to ache your heart bumps, even though it's tough.
You can care all day and still not care enough.

But many people are ego-fetid, hostile, grasping,
        antiromantically dim,
boringly pragmatic, sneaky, too adept at politic party chat:
at least we don't have to feel for them
and thank God for that.

Unless your sympathy is of superhuman amount
it's a mercy that some people don't count.

Horrible

God, yesterday in southern India there was a horrible
earthquake. I just heard it on the radio,
they estimate 23,000 dead. That's interesting news.
I mean 23,000, that's a hell of a lot.
I'm glad it's not 20,000, that would sound sort of
vague and rounded off and unreliable;
23,000 sounds more real and important and serious.
Just think, 23,000 people dying over there
while I was teaching poems by D. H. Lawrence
and having a cherry Danish with Irish Cream coffee.
It was a nice day here, but over there, Jesus!
Not exactly a nice day over there . . . Okay,
here's the *Times*, let's see:
worst earthquake to hit the subcontinent in fifty years,
buildings made of clay collapsed and crushed everybody
wait a second—"death toll may rise as high as ten thousand"—
now that's kind of a let-down, I mean by comparison,
I mean after the radio report
but the radio is probably much more up-to-date
so maybe I won't have to let go of that figure 23,000
which feels nicely impressive and special
and I can think about it when I go out for more coffee
and think, "God, what a world, life is so fragile,
things do happen, things *are* happening, seize the day and
I am definitely not dead."

10-1-93

Taipei Tangle

It was tangled. Policemen stopped a newspaper truck,
two telegrams crossed, an editor laughed too confidently.
Abrupt men in brown jackets moved from the car
to the hotel entrance and stood watching with cigarettes.
The telephone rang in the rear office of the consulate,
a bald man spoke softly into the receiver;
immediately after hanging up he placed another call.
In a humid suburb three Toyotas arrived all at once
outside a ranch-style dwelling that looked normal
and a siren was heard too far to the east.
Printed pages rose like feathers into gray light,
then fell and were trampled by workers and bikes
on the streets of Taipei. History

flowed from its vast sewer out through the hot weather—
gunfire—

though the killers were convicted, certain large questions
went unanswered: Was their target in fact
Liu the double agent or Nan the dissident author?
Which of them had met Rundgren at American Express?
When the news was leaked, what was Chiang thinking
and (more broadly) what sensitivity did Chiang show?
In what sense did Chen Do Ky and the Bamboo Union
act out of patriotism? These were all questions

of some size during the weeks and months of autumn
as the city darkened and oblivious youths strolled
under stoical downtown trees eating shrimp-filled pastry.
Small questions perhaps in the feculent gush of history.
But Helen Liu lies awake listening to taxis,
her eyes shift back and forth much of the night.

Pages

You get this:
October trees durably dark against silver sundown sky
informed
with a sense of the pathos of human beauty.
You have this—for less than a minute . . .

But four years later in a crowded Mexican restaurant
when someone says "My sister lives alone ever since"
your listening is informed
with the black trees of that October minute
and what they printed on a page of soul.
Later, on the network news there's a child in Chicago
who says "My dad needs a job so much." You get
the voice and the worried eyes well informed
about what matters beyond the money,
the father's need to bring it into the chilly house.
The voice is kept, and it finds a subtle paragraph.
Eight years later in Columbus Ohio that file is unerased
at the airport where a father wearing a welders' union cap
reads aloud in lion-voice and warthog-voice
to the girls who nestle beside him—he turns the page
and your soul turns to a dad in Chicago who may by now feel
humorously indispensable, while on the same page
by way of footnote or allusion there's the sister
who learned to live alone

while below noise of travel that airport lounge is shaded
by individual dark trees from twelve Octobers ago

and you keep a shade of this moment
for when someone speaks of airports or daughters or Ohio
or the interest of moving among strangers
two years later in another Mexican restaurant
called The Prickly Pear so the book of your soul gets
pages longer, with these arcane cross-references,
Chicago/Columbus/trees,
unemployment/*The Lion King*/enchiladas,
worried voices/logos on caps/United Airlines/silver sunset.
It needs to be a long book and you'll keep rereading it
for the chance to be well-informed.

Other Pages

(It was not false what he said about the soul,
its accretion of nuanced awareness of human pathos;
for at some level he was as beautifully good
as you are, reader, when you love well;
but there were other pages too,
in that book writing him,
pages edged in a crimson dark whose message was fear

FEAR of the father's thick-browed disappointment
FEAR of the father's voice saying "lazy" and "idiotic"
FEAR of collision with bigger boys their knees their elbows
        their hammy bones their willingness to break noses
FEAR of the fearless sarcastic boys grasping and sucking
        and owning and consuming the idolized girls
FEAR of the girls giggling and whispering away away away
FEAR of being the one deftly disdained by the willowy HER
        and thus forever a forgotten uninvited background figure
        unable to even play a scene matching wits with
        big Death
FEAR of the desert of the mind in the silence after abysmal
        paralyzed isolation at a party

and on each of these pages the last line said
SAVE SELF LET OTHERS FALL

—and it would never not be true that these pages too
were bound into the spine.)

After the Rain

There's a man forty years old dying in Dublin.
No doubt there is also a woman of fifty dying in Bordeaux
and someone only thirty dying near Detroit
but I'm thinking of this man in Dublin dying.

He is listening to a string quartet—Haydn, let us say—
and he hears in it a meaning of sadness
and a sadness of meaning deeper than
the best metaphors I might now produce
if I had the energy which would be a good kind of energy

though maybe not the same as love for my friend
who was almost always, in his healthy years, ironic
about great thoughts. "Let's remember
that even Haydn must have wanted to come out of Haydn,
most days." My friend says
something better than this to someone who soon goes

to answer the phone. Death in a month or two;
rainwater evaporating from Goldsmith Street
seen by my friend from the window upstairs.